D0200533

# ENGLISH CASTLES

### JOHN CURTIS
Text by Richard Ashby

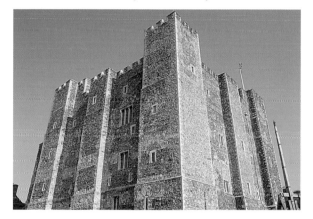

**SALMON**

# INTRODUCTION

The earliest castles were of wood and often made use of the natural features of the landscape. At the centre would be a mound or 'motte' around and below which was the 'bailey', a much larger area surrounded by a wall. Outside was a moat or dry ditch to make the task of storming the walls much more difficult. Later a great tower or 'keep' was built on the motte, a gatehouse with portcullis defended the entrance, and outside that was the 'barbican' which forced the attacker into a confined space, making him vulnerable from above.

As well as having a military purpose, a castle was the home both to its garrison and the Lord and his family. So from the beginning there were living apartments, initially a great hall and later, more sophisticated arrangements giving privacy for the family. There was always a place of worship. In addition the castle was an administrative centre for a wide area; rents were paid here and disputes heard.

Castles have had a variety of fates. Some were 'slighted', that is, partially demolished if their defenders were on the losing side, some were just abandoned and used as a source of stone. For others the domestic side predominated as the country became more peaceful and they are often imposing homes. Whether it is now a picturesque ruin or an impressive stately home the castle has had an important part to play, both in the history of England and its landscape.

Leeds Castle *Kent*

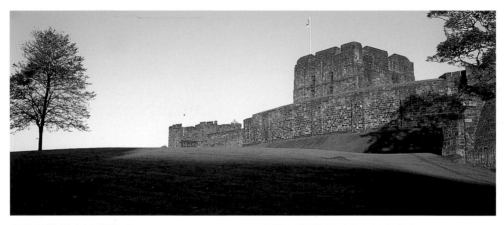

CARLISLE CASTLE *Cumbria*

Carlisle is in the border country and the castle has been at the centre of many conflicts between English and Scots over the centuries. It also played an important part in the English Civil War and in the Jacobite Rebellion of 1745. It is the home to the Border Regiment Museum.

THE TOWER OF LONDON

The central keep or the 'White Tower' along with 'Traitors' Gate', the Crown Jewels, the 'Beefeaters' and the ravens are icons of the tourists' England. A number of English kings used the royal apartments although it was also a prison. Rudolph Hess was held here after his flight to England in 1941.

## TINTAGEL CASTLE *Cornwall*

King Arthur was said to have been born in this castle, and there are associations with Merlin and Tristan and Isolde. The Norman castle, built on a headland which has become isolated from the mainland following sea erosion, was rendered unuseable by the 16th century. Very little remains but it powerfully survives in the imagination and in the legends of King Arthur.

## ROCHESTER CASTLE *Kent*

Rochester was besieged in a major dispute between King John and the Archbishop of Canterbury. Great stone throwing machines failed to breach the walls, which then had to be undermined by sappers digging out the foundations, propping them up with baulks of timber and then setting them alight, bringing down part of a tower. Even then, the garrison did not surrender and they had to be starved into submission.

## CLIFFORD'S TOWER *York*

This is one of two great mottes raised by William the Conqueror either side of the River Ouse, each capped by a wooden tower. In 1190 the Jews of York sought refuge from a riot here but were burnt to death by the mob. This tower replaces a second wooden one and was later named after Robert de Clifford, whose body hung in chains here after his defeat at the Battle of Boroughbridge in 1322.

## ARUNDEL CASTLE *West Sussex*

Arundel Castle, the home of the Dukes of Norfolk, stands on a spur of the South Downs above its town and dominates the meadows and the crossing of the River Arun below. It dates from Norman times and was part of the invaders' strategy for subduing the native English. It was also part of a defensive chain along the south coast against any further invasion across the Channel. It has been besieged three times in its history, twice when its owner rebelled against the ruling king and lastly in the Civil War, when it was held by Royalist forces who suffered a battering by the Parliamentarians. Restorations in the 18th and 19th centuries by the 8th, 11th and, principally, the 15th Dukes of Norfolk have created a remarkable Gothic fantasy, the skyline of which is comparable to that of Windsor.

## BERKELEY CASTLE *Gloucestershire*

Apart from a breach made in the west wall of the keep during a siege by Parliamentary forces in the 17th century, Berkeley is little altered. Its claim to fame is that it was here that the imprisoned King Edward II was so barbarously murdered that his screams were heard in the town nearby, an act so horrific that it has never been forgotten.

## SCARBOROUGH CASTLE *North Yorkshire*

The last bombardment of this Norman castle occurred as late as the First World War when it came under the attack of two German battle-cruisers which had approached under cover of sea mist. The barracks within the castle, which had been constructed after the 1745 Jacobite uprising, were destroyed and many people in the town killed.

HELMSLEY CASTLE *North Yorkshire*
The 12th century founder of this castle,
Walter l'Espec also founded Rievaulx Abbey,
not far away. In Elizabethan times a mansion
was built within the walls. It was besieged by
Parliamentary forces in the Civil War and
after its surrender was slighted and much
of the fortifications destroyed.

PEVENSEY CASTLE *East Sussex*
The Norman invaders re-used and rebuilt the
Roman fort here and Roman walls still survive.
Pevensey was uninhabited by the 16th century
and, apart from a brief revival during the time
of the Armada and the construction of gun
emplacements and pillboxes in the Second
World War, has remained a ruin.

## SCOTNEY CASTLE *Kent*

Scotney is a 14th century fortified manor house rather than a castle, designed for living in rather than for any offensive action. The fortifications were a necessary precaution, though, in a time when this part of England was subject to frequent incursions from the French. It has been much altered and added to in subsequent centuries. The Elizabethans added a south wing which, since the then owner was a Roman Catholic, concealed several priest's holes. The house was searched several times by troops looking for the Jesuit Richard Blount. Much of the 17th century addition has been demolished and, after a new house was built nearby, the castle became a picturesque ruin with the adornment of a lovely garden, famous for its rhododendrons and azaleas.

## TATTERSHALL CASTLE *Lincolnshire*

The great brick tower of Tattershall is the main survival above ground of the castle built by the powerful and rich Lord Treasurer of England, Ralph Lord Cromwell, whose emblem, a purse tied with a cord, is depicted on the great stone fireplaces in the main rooms. Well over a million bricks made from local clay were used in the building of the tower.

## RABY CASTLE *County Durham*

It is thought that the first castle here was built by King Canute, but the present building dates from the 14th century when the powerful Nevill family were given a licence to 'crenellate', that is to fortify, their family house by the Bishop of Durham. The Nevills lost their power after supporting Mary Queen of Scots in the 'Uprising of the North' but the castle is still almost complete.

## WARWICK CASTLE *Warwickshire*

Warwick sits dramatically high above the River Avon, rising from a natural cliff on which a motte was built only two years after the Conquest. The two great towers, 'Caesar's Tower' and 'Guy's Tower', date from the 14th century and dominate both the castle and the surrounding countryside. They were part of an extensive rebuilding and enlargement which largely created the castle we see today.

### KENILWORTH CASTLE *Warwickshire*

Spectacular enough as a ruin today, Kenilworth must have been magnificent when complete, surrounded on all sides by a huge lake. Water defences were always important at Kenilworth and the original, more modest, castle had a moat in which the founder allowed the monks from his priory to fish on Thursdays.

### BARNARD CASTLE *County Durham*

This Norman castle has given its name to the small town which grew up around it. By the early 17th century it had become little more than a source of stone for repairs to Raby Castle nearby and the grounds were being encroached upon by the inhabitants of the town extending their gardens.

## HEVER CASTLE *Kent*

Hever was built in the 13th century as a fortified manor house with a great gateway and bailey and surrounded by a moat. Two hundred years later the Bullen (Boleyn) family built a house inside the walls which was the childhood home of Anne Boleyn. It was here that she was courted by Henry VIII before becoming his second Queen.

## HERSTMONCEUX CASTLE *East Sussex*

This brick castle was built by Sir Roger Fiennes, Henry VI's treasurer, who also owned Hever Castle. After the Second World War it become the home of the Greenwich Observatory, when pollution made its location near London unsuitable. The castle is now a study centre for the Queen's University of Kingston, Ontario, Canada.

## BODIAM CASTLE *East Sussex*

Bodiam is everyone's idea of what a medieval castle should look like. Strong, embattled walls rise out of the wide, flooded moat and the massive gateway with its portcullis is approached across the water by a causeway. It saw little in the way of military action and was practically a ruin by the 15th century, remaining that way until rescued in the 1820s and restored over the next century.

## RICHMOND CASTLE *North Yorkshire*

Richmond provides one of the most complete examples of Norman stone castle building still surviving in the country. It has seen very little military action, being involved in neither the Wars of the Roses nor the English Civil War, and its only function can have been to dominate the principal entrance to Swaledale. By the 16th century it had outlived its usefulness and was left to decay. The curtain wall, enclosing the bailey, follows the triangular shape of its site above the town and there is a steep drop on the south side offering added protection. The keep on the north side is an enlargement of the original gate tower and the castle also has one of the earliest stone built halls, Scolland's Hall, named after the steward of Alan the Red, the original Norman holder of the castle.

## WALMER CASTLE *Kent*

Walmer is one of a line of castles built by Henry VIII as defence against the French. Gunpowder had become important in warfare and so Walmer is low-lying and protected by a moat and earthen ramparts. It has been the official residence of the Lord Warden of the Cinque Ports since the 18th century. The late Queen Mother was a recent Warden.

## LUDLOW CASTLE *Shropshire*

Ludlow was one of the first Norman castles to be built entirely of stone and has an unusual circular chapel within its inner courtyard. Henry VII, the first Tudor king and a Welshman by birth, spent much of his early life here and his son and heir, Arthur, also lived here with his wife Catherine of Aragon who, on Arthur's death married his brother, Henry VIII.

### WINDSOR CASTLE *Berkshire*

The Royal Standard flies over Windsor Castle whenever the Queen is in residence. It is the largest occupied castle in the world and its silhouette is familiar to millions. It is a huge castle and a Royal Palace. Much altered and extended by successive monarchs, it still retains a medieval appearance.

### COLCHESTER CASTLE *Essex*

Built on the foundation vaults of the Temple of Claudius, Colchester Castle was constructed from the brick and stone of the surrounding Roman ruins. Although it was held by the French for three months in the 13th century it has seen little military action and is now the home of the Colchester and Essex Museum.

## FRAMLINGHAM CASTLE *Suffolk*

Framlingham is a shell standing high above its little town. All that remains is the curtain wall but this is complete with thirteen open-backed towers. Visitors can walk all the way around the wall today. Curiously, most of the Tudor elaborately patterned brick chimneys rising from many of the towers are dummies. Henry VIII gave Framlingham to his daughter Mary and she was staying here when the Earl of Arundel brought the news that she was Queen of England. Under her sister, Elizabeth I, the castle was mostly used to imprison Roman Catholic priests who refused to adhere to the new Church of England. In the 17th century almost all the buildings inside the wall were pulled down and a Poorhouse built instead. This building subsequently became a courtroom, a meeting hall and then the parish fire station.

## CASTLE RISING *Norfolk*

Here only the 12th century keep survives. It is remarkably intact, with good Norman carving. Though there are some remains of the gatehouse and the chapel, the outer walls are long gone. Isabella, Edward II's queen, known as the 'She-wolf of France', was held here for the last thirty years of her life after her trial for the murder of her husband at Berkeley Castle in 1327.

## BAMBURGH CASTLE *Northumberland*

Standing on a volcanic outcrop dominating the surrounding countryside with a sheer drop into the sea, this place has long been fortified. The castle was a centre of considerable resistance to the Norman invaders and was besieged by William II in 1095. It played its part in the Wars of the Roses and was the first English castle to be badly damaged by cannon.

Published in Great Britain by J. Salmon Ltd., Sevenoaks, Kent TN13 1BB. Telephone 01732 452381. Email enquiries@jsalmon.co.uk
Design by John Curtis. Text and photographs © John Curtis All rights reserved. No part of this book may be produced, stored in a retrieval system or transmitted in any form or by any means without prior written permission of the publishers.
ISBN 1-902842-64-2   Printed in Italy © 2005

Title page photograph: Dover Castle *Kent.*
Front cover photograph: Corfe Castle *Dorset.*   Back cover photograph: Portchester Castle *Hampshire*